QUILTING WITH
precuts AND shortcuts

TERRY MARTIN

Martingale®
& C O M P A N Y

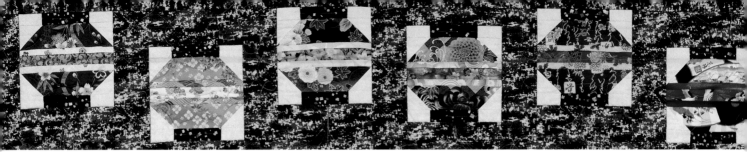

Quilting with Precuts and Shortcuts
© 2010 by Terry Martin

That Patchwork Place® is an imprint
of Martingale & Company®.

Martingale & Company
20205 144th Ave. NE
Woodinville, WA 98072-8478 USA
www.martingale-pub.com

Printed in China
15 14 13 12 11 10   8 7 6 5 4 3 2 1

Library of Congress Cataloging-in-Publication Data is available upon request.

ISBN: 978-1-56477-995-3

Mission Statement

Dedicated to providing quality products and service to inspire creativity.

Credits

President & CEO: Tom Wierzbicki

Editor in Chief: Mary V. Green

Managing Editor: Tina Cook

Developmental Editor: Karen Costello Soltys

Technical Editor: Laurie Baker

Copy Editor: Sheila Chapman Ryan

Design Director: Stan Green

Production Manager: Regina Girard

Illustrator: Adrienne Smitke

Cover & Text Designer: Regina Girard

Photographer: Brent Kane

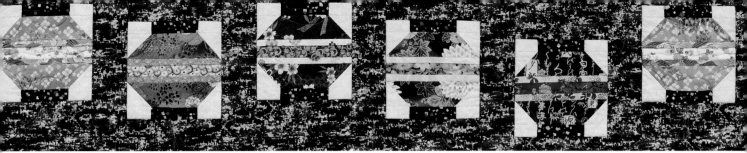

DEDICATION

I would like to dedicate this book to my husband, Ed. You make my life easy. I thank you and I love you, always and forever.

ACKNOWLEDGMENTS

I've said it before but it really *does* take a village to write a book. Many thanks go to my family members who are always willing to share their opinion on color and fabrics, and to my best friend, Cornelia, who adds a second pair of eyes for me to see through.

Many thanks to my extraordinary machine quilters who add that extra dimension of design to my quilts: Adrienne Reynolds, the coolest, who came to my rescue when due dates came up way too fast; Barb Dau, one of the most talented machine quilters ever; Karen Burns, who has a wonderful whimsical style; and Sue Lohse, the fastest machine quilter I know. You are all fabulous! You may contact Adrienne Reynolds at Artichoke Quilts, 425-870-6719, or artiquilts@verizon.net.

And, of course, another round of thanks to the staff at Martingale & Company and especially my editor, Laurie Baker.

CONTENTS

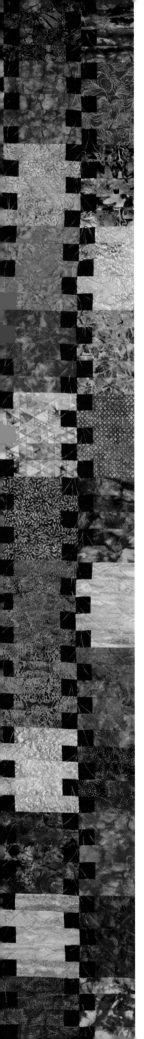

INTRODUCTION

I like to sew, and I really like to sew quilts. And sometimes I don't have the time, patience, or willingness to sew complicated quilts. Sometimes I just like to cut simple strips, squares, triangles, and rectangles and sew. I'm betting I'm not the only one. Hence, this book.

I also like to make things easy on myself, especially when I just want to sit and sew. But at the same time I don't want to make boring quilts. I like the creativity of making something beautiful and easy at the same time! Now I know what you're thinking: "If it's going to be easy and simple, it's going to look that way." Stop right there and get out of that mindset! You see, I have crowned myself the Queen of Easy Quilts! That means that I have taken all the comforts of the modern age of quilting—ready-cut squares and strips, fat quarters, rotary cutters and rulers, fusible appliqué, and so on—and put them to good use in making pretty, fun, and easy quilts!

The projects in this book are divided into three categories based on the fast and easy cutting and piecing methods I use to reduce time at the cutting and sewing table but that guarantee success. I've even thrown in a couple of shortcuts that will excite your creativity. I know these methods work, based on my best friend Cornelia's experience. Poor Cornelia was a frustrated piecer/quilter for a long time. She would get bogged down with a project and question her ability, and at one time she thought of quitting quilting altogether! Yikes, I really felt for her! Then she took a look at what was making her so frustrated and eliminated it. She is now the self-proclaimed Pointless Piecing Princess. She wanted the joy of making quilts without the "hard" parts to get in the way. She now makes easy quilts and they're beautiful. She's happy and that's all that matters.

This is what I wish for all of you: to make simple quilts that are fun, beautiful, and that make you happy.

Cheers!

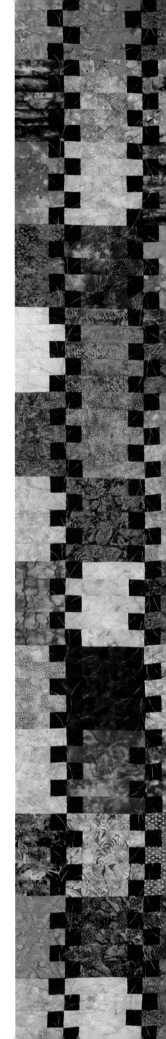

special METHODS

Here are some of my techniques to simplify quiltmaking. Stacking fabrics so they can be cut all at once, strip piecing, and chain stitching are all super-easy techniques that reduce time and frustration yet yield pretty quilts.

Use Fabulous Fabrics for Dynamic Results

I love, love, love fabric! Designing easy quilts is all about quick methods and terrific results, but you can't ignore the fabric! These quilt designs let the fabrics really take center stage. Batiks, Asian prints, soft romantic florals, modern hip designs, '60s retro, or Hawaiian prints—you name it, I like it, and they all look great in these quilts. Did I mention that I love fabric? These quilt designs and methods give you the opportunity to stretch your imagination with fabric. Fabric prints and colors you may not use every day can be a lot of fun to work with using these designs. I let the fabric "talk" to me. (Sometimes I talk back but my family and friends have learned to just ignore the crazy quilting lady!) Are the prints too large to cut up in small pieces? Do they need to be calmed down or punched up a bit? More often than not I design my quilts after I have selected the focus fabric.

Put it this way—because you don't have to put a huge investment of time and energy into these quilts, you can take the opportunity to play around with fabulous fabrics that you may not normally use!

Sew with Precut Pieces

Using precut fabric is a great way to dive into a project. With coordinating bundles of fat quarters (18" x 20" rectangles), charm squares (5" squares), Jelly Rolls (2½"-wide strips), Layer Cakes (10" squares), Honey Buns (1½"-wide strips), and Turnovers (6" triangles), such as created by Moda, a lot of the cutting is done for you. (Sheesh, I'm suddenly hungry for pastries!) Many of these fabric bundles are cut from one collection of fabric, so it's a great way to work with an entire line. I used several of these precut collections in the projects.

If you have a little bit of extra time, it's fun to create your own bundles of pieces from yardage and then trade them with friends and guild members for really scrappy quilts!

Sewing with precut strips and squares is one of the fastest methods I know for quickly completing a quilt. I belong to a guild that trades 6" squares every month. Each month is a different theme, so you can pick and choose which types of fabrics you want to exchange. My guild began exchanging squares long before the fabric manufacturers provided their time-saving packages, and I can't tell you how many times I've pulled out my bin of squares for a project.

Stack and Cut for Fast Results

When several fabrics need to be cut to the same size, stack the fabrics and cut them all at once. I'm able to accurately cut through eight layers of fabric at one time, but if that's too many layers for you to comfortably cut through, even half that many layers will still cut down your cutting time. If you're a beginner (this book is perfect for you!), practice cutting multiple layers at one time, making sure you follow the "inchworm" technique I've outlined on page 57 so that your cuts are accurate.

Save Time with Strip Sets

Simplifying the sewing process is next, and sewing strips of fabric together along the long edges to create strip sets is one of the easiest ways to cut down on your piecing time. Rather than sewing a specific sequence of pieces together over and over again, strips of fabric are sewn together, and then cut into segments. These segments are sewn back together in a particular arrangement to create the design.

Sewing strip sets together is what I call idiot sewing. I know, it doesn't sound pretty, but that's how I describe it for myself. There are times I don't want to have to think too much about what I'm stitching, like when I know I'm going to be interrupted by family, pets, or the phone, or when I'm at a quilting retreat where I'll be chatting a lot. These are the times I need to do a task I don't have to think about too much. The simple task of sewing strip after strip together allows me to get a lot

done without a lot of risk of messing up. And because I can complete a lot in just a little amount of time, it keeps me motivated so I can get to the next step.

As with any piecing technique, make sure you're stitching an accurate ¼" seam allowance, and don't tug or pull your fabric through the machine, which can lead to stretched seams that pucker or bow.

Piece and Appliqué with Simple Shapes

I love to use simple shapes in my quilts. Piecing with simple shapes ensures the best results when matching seams, and perfectly matched seams lead to little need for easing, which in turn leads to flatter, squarer quilts. Along with simple squares and rectangles, I really like using quarter-square triangles to make Hourglass blocks for my designs. Cutting quarter-square triangles is easily done by cutting a square into quarters diagonally. When four triangles are rejoined, they are stitched in such a manner that the center seam locks into place, guaranteeing perfectly matched seams. Focus on the center seam when piecing this fun block; the outer edges will fall into place or you can manipulate them if necessary.

I also like to use basic shapes when I do fusible appliqué. It's a real confidence booster to be able to easily topstitch around simple shapes, not to mention how much easier they are to cut out than complex ones!

Make Template-Free Fusible Appliqués

I love the look of appliqué, but traditional methods often take more time than I want. While the results of traditional methods are very satisfying, every once in a while I just need something that gets the job done quickly while still enhancing the project. For those quilts, I use fusible-web appliqué methods and simple shapes. Just freehand cut the shape from a piece of fabric onto which fusible web has been applied, and then follow the manufacturer's instructions to fuse them in place. I did this for "Charming Squares and Diamonds" on page 48. I wanted to add some interest to a small charm-square quilt that I had sewed together that was cute by itself but needed something extra. A friend from my guild, Judy Irish, showed me how she had fused simple diamond shapes over a pieced background, and the results were amazing! The quilt looked like it had been put together with complicated piecing but it hadn't. I wanted to create the same look on my charm quilt. I knew the size of the diamond shape should be the same size as the length of the finished block; I figured out how to cut the diamonds freehand so that no templates were needed. The results were fantastic and very easy!

Charming Squares and Diamonds

Not only is this a great way to add extra dimension to your quilts, but appliqués can also hide a multitude of "sins." If you are a beginning quilter, sometimes your seams don't exactly match at every intersection. When you add appliqué over the seams, no one knows they didn't match, and you have a great looking quilt. I covered the seams with appliqués on both "Charming Squares and Diamonds" and "Flower Power" on page 51.

Flower Power

indonesian RAILROAD

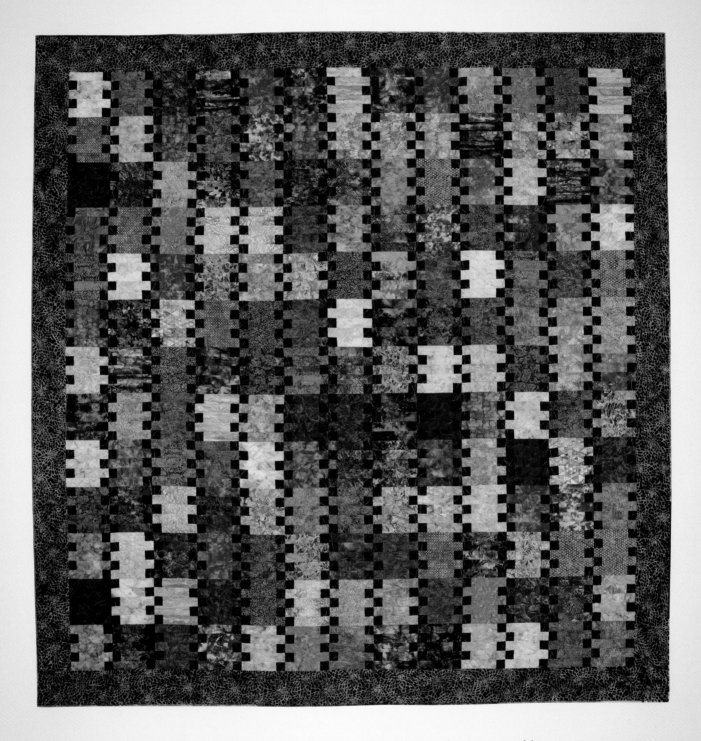

By Terry Martin. Machine quilted by the creative Adrienne Reynolds.

Finished quilt: 109½" x 109½" • **Finished block:** 7½" x 7½"

I think this is the easiest quilt I've ever designed and made! Using batiks was a no-brainer; I love their dimensional look and rich colors. One strip set will make four blocks. Simply crosscut the strip sets, rotate every other segment, and stitch them back together. You can make this quilt any size you want, from table topper to lap quilt to king size, like this one.

Materials

Yardage is based on 42"-wide fabric.

$8\frac{7}{8}$ yards *total* of assorted batiks for blocks

$2\frac{5}{8}$ yards of dark blue print for blocks

$2\frac{1}{4}$ yards of blue batik for border

$\frac{7}{8}$ yard of fabric for binding (I used leftover strips of the assorted batiks)

$9\frac{3}{4}$ yards of fabric for backing

114" x 114" piece of batting

Cutting

All measurements include ¼"-wide seam allowances.

From the assorted batiks, cut a *total* of:
43 strips, 6½" x 42"

From the dark blue print, cut:
43 strips, 2" x 42"

From the blue batik, cut:
11 strips, 6½" x 42"

From the binding fabric, cut:
11 strips, 2¼" x 42"

Making the Blocks

1 Sew a dark blue print strip to one long edge of each assorted batik strip. Make 43 strip sets. Press the seam allowances toward the blue print. Crosscut *each* strip set into 20 segments, 2" wide. Stack the strip sets for quick cutting.

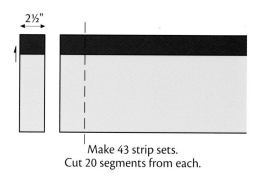

Make 43 strip sets.
Cut 20 segments from each.

2 Sew five identical segments together, rotating the segments as shown to make the design. Repeat to make a total of 169 blocks. You will have enough segments left over to make three additional blocks, if desired.

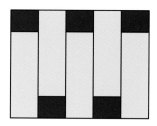

Make 169 total.

Assembling the Quilt Top

1   Refer to the quilt assembly diagram to arrange the blocks into 13 rows of 13 blocks each, making sure the dark blue squares alternate.

2   Sew the blocks in each row together. Press the seam allowances in alternate directions from row to row. Sew the rows together. Press the seam allowances in one direction.

3   Refer to "Adding Borders" on page 59 to add the border to the quilt top using the blue batik 6½"-wide strips.

Finishing the Quilt

1   Layer the quilt top with batting and backing. Baste the layers together.

2   Hand or machine quilt as desired.

3   Square up the quilt sandwich.

4   Prepare and sew the binding to the quilt using the 2¼"-wide strips of binding fabric. Add a hanging sleeve, if desired, and a label.

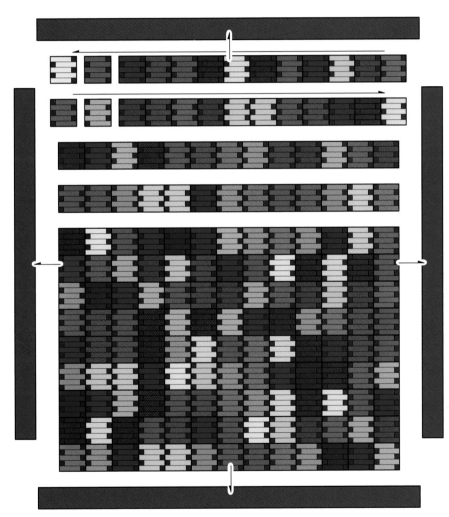

Quilt assembly

easy peasy, ONE TWO THREESY

By Terry Martin. Machine quilted by the incomparable Adrienne Reynolds.

Finished quilt: 48" x 48" • **Finished blocks:** 6" x 6", 8" x 8", and 18" x 18"

I'm a sucker for a great striped fabric, and these Kaffe Fassett–styled stripes were irresistible! I had a fat-quarter pack of them, and when I combined them with solid batiks, a richly colored, fun, and playful quilt emerged. This would be great for a baby gift or a dorm room that needs some pizzazz.

Materials

Yardage is based on 42"-wide fabric.

1 fat quarter *each* of batik solids in pink, blue, yellow, green, light orange, olive green, and peach for blocks

1 fat quarter *each* of multicolored striped homespun fabrics with the dominant stripes in green, yellow, orange, and pink for blocks

1 fat quarter *each* of plaid homespun fabrics in blue-and-green, purple-and-pink, orange-and-yellow, and purple-and-orange for blocks

⅝ yard of multicolored batik for blocks and binding

2 fat quarters of multicolored striped homespun with the dominant stripe in blue for blocks

¼ yard of orange-pink-and-yellow batik for inner border

1 fat quarter of batik for quilt center block

3 yards of fabric for backing

52" x 52" piece of batting

Cutting

All measurements include ¼"-wide seam allowances.

From the batik fat quarter for center block, cut:

1 square, 12½" x 12½"

From the blue multicolored striped homespun fat quarters, cut:

8 strips, 1½" x 20"; crosscut into:
  4 rectangles, 1½" x 4½"
  10 rectangles, 1½" x 6½"
  6 rectangles, 1½" x 8½"
2 strips, 2½" x 12½"
2 strips, 2½" x 16½"
3 squares, 4½" x 4½"

From the multicolored batik, cut:

5 strips, 1½" x 42"; crosscut into:
  2 strips, 1½" x 16½"
  2 strips, 1½" x 18½"
  6 strips, 1½" x 6½"
  6 strips, 1½" x 8½"
5 strips, 2¼" x 42"

From *each* of the 4 multicolored plaid homespun fat quarters, cut:

5 strips, 2½" x 20" (20 total)

From *each* of the solid yellow, green, light orange, and peach batiks, cut:

3 strips, 2½" x 20" (12 total)

From the solid pink batik fat quarter, cut:

3 squares, 4½" x 4½"
7 strips, 1½" x 20"; crosscut into:
  2 rectangles, 1½" x 4½"
  8 rectangles, 1½" x 6½"
  6 rectangles, 1½" x 8½"

From the pink multicolored striped homespun fat quarter, cut:

1 square, 4½" x 4½"
6 strips, 1½" x 20"; crosscut into:
  6 rectangles, 1½" x 4½"
  8 rectangles, 1½" x 6½"
  2 rectangles, 1½" x 8½"

From the solid olive green batik fat quarter, cut:

2 squares, 4½" x 4½"
7 strips, 1½" x 20"; crosscut into:
  6 rectangles, 1½" x 4½"
  10 rectangles, 1½" x 6½"
  4 rectangles, 1½" x 8½"

From the solid blue batik fat quarter, cut:

2 squares, 4½" x 4½"

7 strips, 1½" x 20"; crosscut into:

    6 rectangles, 1½" x 4½"

    10 rectangles, 1½" x 6½"

    4 rectangles, 1½" x 8½"

From *each* of the green and yellow multicolored striped homespun fat quarters, cut:

3 squares, 4½" x 4½"

8 strips, 1½" x 20"; crosscut into:

    4 rectangles, 1½" x 4½"

    10 rectangles, 1½" x 6½"

    6 rectangles, 1½" x 8½"

From the remainder of the solid light orange batik fat quarter, cut:

3 squares, 4½" x 4½"

4 strips, 1½" x 20"; crosscut into:

    6 rectangles, 1½" x 4½"

    6 rectangles, 1½" x 6½"

From the orange multicolored striped homespun fat quarter, cut:

3 squares, 4½" x 4½"

9 strips, 1½" x 20"; crosscut into:

    6 rectangles, 1½" x 4½"

    12 rectangles, 1½" x 6½"

    6 rectangles, 1½" x 8½"

From the orange-pink-and-yellow batik for inner border, cut:

2 strips, 1½" x 30½"

2 strips, 1½" x 32½"

Making the Blocks

1 For the center block, sew the blue multicolored striped 2½" x 12½" strips to the sides of the 12½" x 12½" center square. Press the seam allowances toward the center square. Sew the blue multicolored striped 2½" x 16½" strips to the top and bottom of the center square. Press the seam allowances toward the center square. In the same manner, add the multicolored batik 1½" x 16½" strips to the sides of the previous unit and the multicolored batik 1½" x 18½" strips to the top and bottom, pressing toward the center square after each addition.

2 To make the Nine Patch blocks, group the five 2½" x 20" strips cut from each homespun plaid color with the three 2½" x 20" strips cut from a coordinating batik solid. You will have a total of four color groups. For each color group, sew a plaid strip to both long edges of a solid strip to make strip set A. Repeat to make a total of two strip sets. Press the seam allowances toward the plaid strips. Crosscut the strip sets into eight segments, 2½" wide. Sew the remaining solid strips to both long edges of the remaining plaid strip to make strip set B. Press the seam allowances toward the plaid strip. Crosscut the strip set into four segments, 2½" wide.

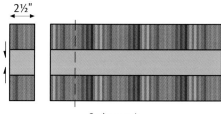

2½"

Strip set A.
Make 2 from each color group.
Cut 8 segments from each.

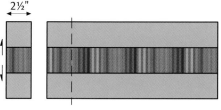

2½"

Strip set B.
Make 1 from each color group.
Cut 4 segments from each.

3 Using the segments from the same color group, sew an A segment to the sides of a B segment. Repeat to make four blocks from each color group (16 total).

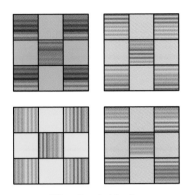

Nine Patch blocks.
Make 4 blocks from each color group.

4 To make the White House Steps blocks, group the squares and rectangles from the following fabrics together: solid pink batik and multicolored pink stripe; solid olive green batik and multicolored blue stripe; solid blue batik and multicolored yellow stripe; and finally the solid light orange batik, multicolored orange stripe, and the remaining multicolored batik 1½"-wide rectangles. For each of the groupings, sew rectangles of the opposite fabric to each square. Start by adding the 4½"-long rectangles to the sides, and then add the 6½"-long rectangles to the top and bottom. Add rectangles of fabric that are the same as the center square to each of these units, adding the 6½"-long rectangles to the sides and the 8½"-long rectangles to the top and bottom. For the blocks with a light orange center square, use the multicolored batik rectangles around the outside of the block. Make a total of 10 blocks with solid square centers and 10 blocks with striped square centers.

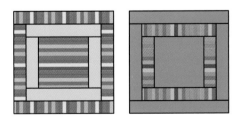

White House Steps blocks.
Make 10 each.

Assembling the Quilt Top

1 Using a design wall (mine is the floor!), arrange the Nine Patch blocks around the center block so that the dominant stripes are vertical, placing three along each side and five across the top and bottom. When you're pleased with the color arrangement, rotate every other block so that the dominant stripes are horizontal. Sew the three blocks along each side together to make two rows. Join these rows to the sides of the center block. Press the seam allowances toward the quilt center. Sew the five blocks along the top and bottom together to make two rows. Add these rows to the top and bottom of the center block. Press the seam allowances toward the quilt center.

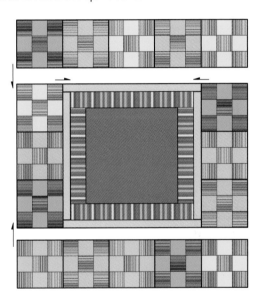

2 Sew the orange-pink-and-yellow batik 1½" x 30½" strips to the sides of the quilt top. Press the seam allowances toward the strips. Sew the orange-pink-and-yellow 1½" x 32½" strips to the top and bottom of the quilt top. Press the seam allowances toward the strips.

3 Place your quilt top on your design wall and arrange the White House blocks around the quilt, alternating the blocks with striped and solid center squares. Place four blocks along each side and six blocks across the top and bottom. When you're pleased with the arrangement, sew the four blocks along each side together to make two rows. Join these to the sides of the quilt top. Press the seam allowances toward the quilt center. Sew the six blocks along the top and bottom together to make two rows. Add these rows to the top and bottom of the quilt top. Press the seam allowances toward the quilt center.

Finishing the Quilt

1 Layer the quilt top with batting and backing. Baste the layers together.

2 Hand or machine quilt as desired.

3 Square up the quilt sandwich.

4 Prepare and sew the binding to the quilt using the multicolored batik 2¼"-wide strips. Add a hanging sleeve, if desired, and a label.

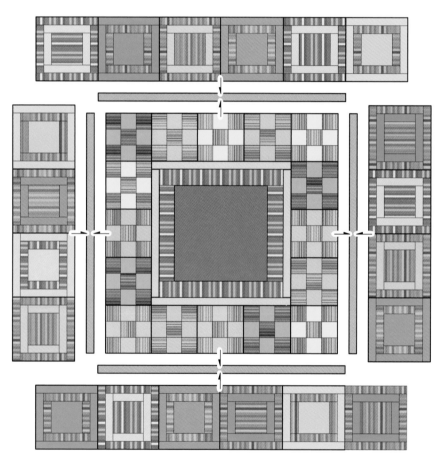

Quilt assembly

chinese LANTERNS

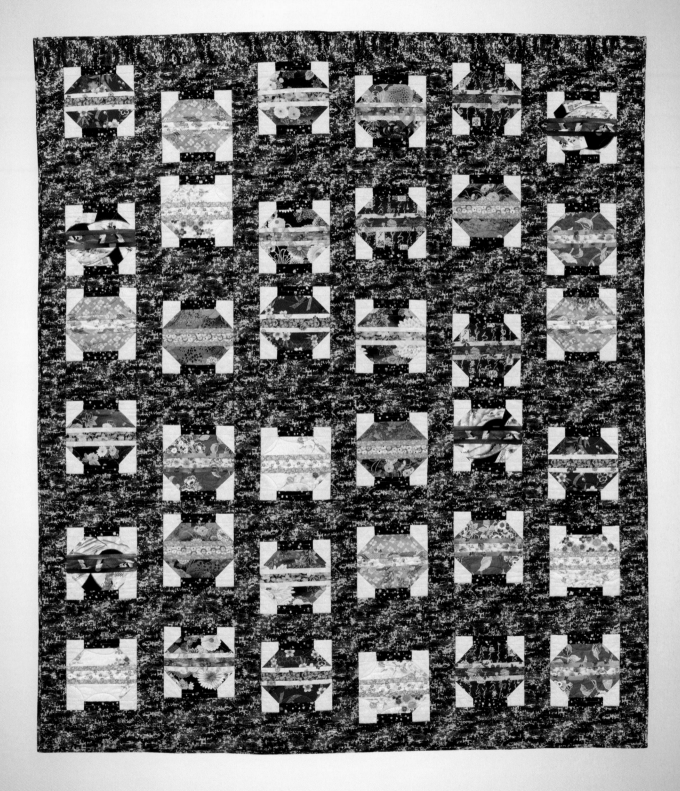

By Terry Martin. Machine quilted by the incredible Karen Burns.

Finished quilt: 69" x 79½" • **Finished block:** 8" x 11"

I teach once a month at the Quiltmaker's Shoppe in Arlington, Washington. The class is called Soup 'n' Sew; I provide the project of the month, the owners make homemade soup, a couple of students bring fresh-baked bread, and we all have a great time gabbing and sewing. The project is a block or small project that can be finished during the class, with the students getting fabric and cutting instructions ahead of time. This Chinese Lantern block was a student favorite. It's super easy because it's strip pieced; each strip set makes four blocks. Plus the narrow accent strips are actually folded strips of fabric that give the block dimension. So, grab your stash of Asian fabrics or pretty florals and let's get busy!

Materials

Yardage is based on 42"-wide fabric.

3½ yards of black-and-gold print for sashing, borders, and binding

¼ yard *each* of 9 assorted prints for lantern main pieces*

1¼ yards of cream print for block backgrounds

⅛ yard *each* of 9 assorted prints for lantern center strips*

⅛ yard *each* of 9 assorted prints for lantern accent strips*

½ yard of black print for lantern top and bottom rims

4¾ yards of fabric for backing

75" x 86" piece of batting

Each lantern main fabric should coordinate with a center-strip fabric and an accent fabric.

Cutting

All measurements include ¼"-wide seam allowances.

From *each* of the 9 assorted prints for lantern accent strips, cut:

2 strips, 1½" x 42" (18 total)

From *each* of the 9 assorted prints for lantern center strips, cut:

1 strip, 2½" x 42" (9 total)

From *each* of the 9 assorted prints for lantern main pieces, cut:

2 strips, 2½" x 42" (18 total)

From the cream print, cut:

15 strips, 2½" x 42"; crosscut 9 strips into 144 squares, 2½" x 2½"

From the black print, cut:

3 strips, 4½" x 42"

From the black-and-gold print, cut:

24 strips, 3½" x 42"; crosscut 16 strips into:
  24 rectangles, 3½" x 8½"
  30 rectangles, 3½" x 11½"
6 strips, 2" x 42"; crosscut into 24 rectangles, 2" x 8½"
8 strips, 2½" x 42"

Making the Blocks

1 Press the lantern accent 1½" x 42" strips in half lengthwise, wrong sides together.

2 Select a 2½" x 42" center strip and place it right side up on your work surface. Position an accent strip along one long edge of the center strip, aligning the raw edges. With the wrong side up, layer a lantern main 2½" x 42" strip over the pieces. Make sure the raw edges of all three pieces are aligned along the same long edge. Stitch the strips together along this edge. Press the seam allowance toward the center strip. When you press from the right side, make sure the accent strip is pressed toward the center strip. Repeat on the opposite long edge of

the center strip using matching accent and main print strips. Repeat to make a total of nine strip sets. Crosscut each strip set into four segments, 8½" wide.

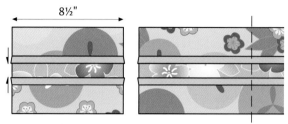

Make 1 strip set from each of the 9 sets of coordinating fabrics. Cut 4 segments from each.

3 Using a sharp pencil or fabric marker, draw a diagonal line from corner to corner on the wrong side of each cream print 2½" square. Position a square on each corner of a segment from step 2, paying careful attention to the direction of the marked lines. Stitch on the lines. Trim ¼" from the stitching lines. Press the resulting triangles toward the corners. Repeat to make a total of 36 units.

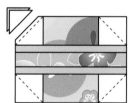

Make 36.

4 Sew cream print 2½" x 42" strips to both long edges of a black print 4½" x 42" strip to make a strip set. Press the seam allowances toward the black print strip. Repeat to make a total of three strip sets. Crosscut the strip sets into 72 segments, 1½" wide.

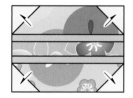

Make 3 strip sets.
Cut 72 segments.

5 Sew segments from step 4 to the top and bottom of each unit from step 3.

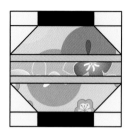 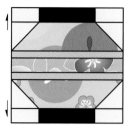

Make 36.

6 Sew a black-and-gold print 3½" x 8½" rectangle to the bottom of 24 of the units from step 5 to make block A. Sew black-and-gold print 2" x 8½" rectangles to the top and bottom of the remaining 12 blocks from step 5 to make block B.

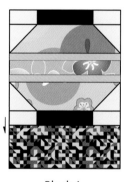 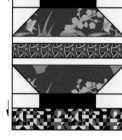

Block A.
Make 24.

Block B.
Make 12.

Assembling the Quilt Top

1 Refer to the quilt assembly diagram on page 22 or randomly arrange the blocks into six rows of six blocks each so the lanterns look like they're moving up and down. When you're pleased with the arrangement, sew the blocks in each row together, inserting a black-and-gold-print 3½" x 11½" vertical sashing rectangle between the blocks.

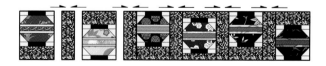

2   Sew the black-and-gold print 3½" x 42" strips together end to end to make one long strip. Measure across a block row and cut five horizontal sashing strips to this measurement from the pieced strip. Sew the rows together, inserting a sashing strip between the rows.

3   Refer to "Adding Borders" on page 59 to add the border to the quilt top using the remaining black-and-gold print 3½"-wide strips.

Finishing the Quilt

1   Layer the quilt top with batting and backing. Baste the layers together.

2   Hand or machine quilt as desired.

3   Square up the quilt sandwich.

4   Prepare and sew the binding to the quilt using the black-and-gold print 2½"-wide strips. Add a hanging sleeve, if desired, and a label.

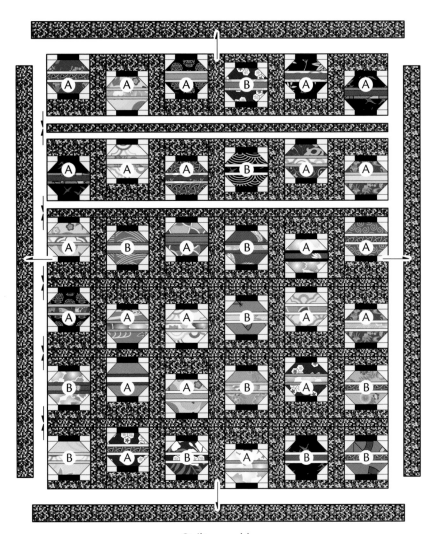

Quilt assembly

beautiful BABIES

By Terry Martin.

Finished quilt: 59" x 63½" • **Finished block:** 7" x 7"

I originally planned this quilt to be a small doll quilt using 3" squares, but when I found this adorable baby print in my stash I had to enlarge the blocks to show off the fabric. The batiks give a kick to the traditional baby quilt. Please note that the baby print is directional and I had to take care to make sure all the babies were right side up. If you are using a directional print, take care to place the orange and blue strips on the theme print correctly.

Materials

Yardage is based on 42"-wide fabric.

1¾ yards of blue batik for blocks and outer border

1⅛ yards of baby print for blocks

⅝ yard of yellow print for blocks and inner border

⅝ yard of orange batik for blocks

½ yard of fabric for binding

3⅞ yards of fabric for backing

66" x 73" piece of batting

Cutting

All measurements include ¼"-wide seam allowances.

From the baby print, cut:
6 strips, 5½" x 42"

From the orange batik, cut:
3 strips, 2½" x 42"
2 strips, 5½" x 42"

From the blue batik, cut:
3 strips, 2½" x 42"
2 strips, 5½" x 42"
6 strips, 6½" x 42"

From the yellow print, cut:
4 strips, 2½" x 42"
5 strips, 1¾" x 42"

From the binding fabric, cut:
7 strips, 2¼" x 42"

Making the Blocks

1 Sew a baby print 5½" x 42" strip to each orange batik and blue batik 2½" x 42" strip to make strips sets A and B. Make three of each. Press the seam allowances toward the batik strips. Stack the A strip sets and then crosscut into 21 segments, 5½" wide. Repeat with the B strip sets.

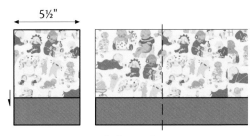

5½"

Strip set A.
Make 3. Cut 21 segments.

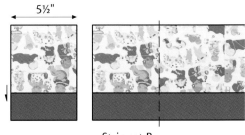

5½"

Strip set B.
Make 3. Cut 21 segments.

2 Sew the yellow print 2½" x 42" strips to each orange batik and blue batik 5½" x 42" strip to make strip sets C and D. Press the seam allowances toward the batik strips. Make two of each. Stack the C strip sets and then crosscut into 21 segments, 2½" wide. Repeat with the D strip sets.

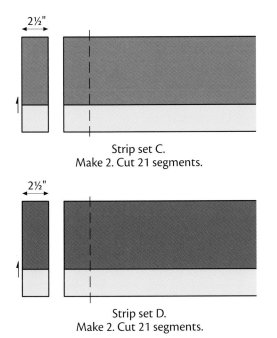

2½"

Strip set C.
Make 2. Cut 21 segments.

2½"

Strip set D.
Make 2. Cut 21 segments.

3 Sew a C segment to each A segment as shown. Sew a D segment to each B segment as shown.

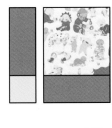

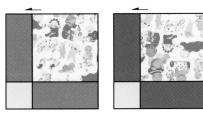

Make 21 of each.

Assembling the Quilt Top

1 Refer to the quilt assembly diagram below to arrange the blocks into seven rows of six blocks each, alternating and rotating the blocks within each row and from row to create the pattern. Sew the blocks in each row together. Press the seam allowances in opposite directions from row to row. Sew the rows together. Press the seam allowances in one direction.

2 Refer to "Adding Borders" on page 59 to add the inner border using the yellow 1¾"-wide strips. Repeat to add the outer border using the blue batik 6½"-wide strips.

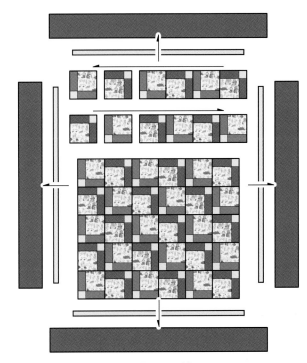

Quilt assembly

Finishing the Quilt

1 Layer the quilt top with batting and backing. Baste the layers together.

2 Hand or machine quilt as desired.

3 Square up the quilt sandwich.

4 Prepare and sew the binding to the quilt using the 2¼"-wide strips of binding fabric. Add a hanging sleeve, if desired, and a label.

strip-pieced PUZZLE

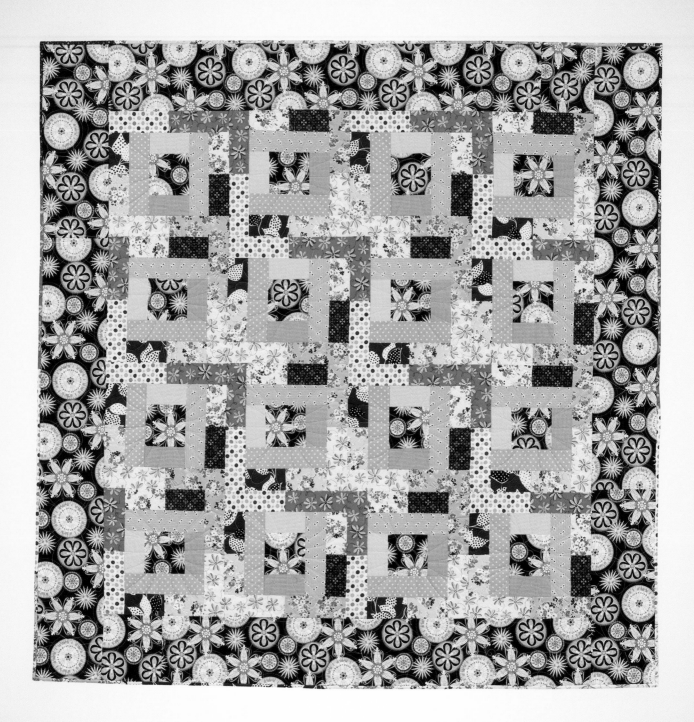

By Terry Martin. Machine quilted by the fantabulous Adrienne Reynolds.

Finished quilt: 61" x 61" • **Finished block:** 12" x 12"

This block is called Crayon Box, and I really like it because it has so many possibilities. I decided to make a controlled scrappy quilt with this block. Controlled scrappy means that there is a different fabric in each segment of the block but the blocks are all the same. Your eye wanders over the quilt but you get a sense of unity from the repeated color placement. This quilt is easy to make using strip piecing.

Materials

Yardage is based on 42"-wide fabric.

13 assorted fat quarters for blocks and binding*

1⅓ yards of multicolored print for border**

4 yards of fabric for backing

67" x 67" piece of batting

Fat quarters must measure at least 18" x 20"

**If you want to use this fabric for the center of your blocks (fabric 1) as I did, purchase 1⅝ yards and eliminate one of the fat quarters.*

Cutting

All measurements include ¼"-wide seam allowances. This is a controlled scrappy block, so for best results, audition the fat quarters for each of the 13 segments of the block, referring to the block diagram below. When you have determined the position of each fabric, number the fabrics with their respective position in the block.

```
 ┌──────────┬──────────┐
 │    10    │    11    │
 ├───┬──────┴───┬──────┤
 │   │    2     │      │
 │ 6 ├────┬─────┤  8   │
 │   │    │     │      │
 ├───┤ 4  │ 1 │ 5│      │
 │ 7 │    │     │  9   │
 │   ├────┴─────┤      │
 │   │    3     │      │
 ├───┴──────┬───┴──────┤
 │    12    │    13    │
 └──────────┴──────────┘
```

From fabric 1, cut:

4 strips, 4½" x the longest edge of the fat quarter

From *each* of fabrics 2 and 3, cut:

4 strips, 2½" x the longest edge of the fat quarter (8 total)

From *each* of fabrics 4 and 5, cut:

8 strips, 2½" x the shortest edge of the fat quarter; crosscut into 16 rectangles, 2½" x 8½" (32 total)

From *each* of fabrics 6–9, cut:

2 strips, 4½" x the longest edge of the fat quarter (8 total)

From *each* of fabrics 10–13, cut:

2 strips, 6½" x the longest edge of the fat quarter (8 total)

From the multicolored print, cut:

6 strips, 7" x 42"

From the remainder of the fat quarters, cut a *total* of:

13 strips, 2½" wide

Making the Blocks

1 Sew one strip each of fabrics 2 and 3 to opposite long edges of a fabric 1 strip to make strip set A. Repeat to make a total of four strip sets. Press the seam allowances toward fabrics 2 and 3. Crosscut the strip sets into 16 segments, 4½" wide.

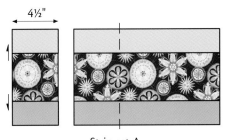

4½"

Strip set A.
Make 4. Cut 16 segments.

2 To each A segment from step 1, sew a fabric 4 rectangle to the left edge and a fabric 5 rectangle to the right edge. Press the seam allowances away from the A segments.

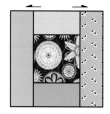

Make 16.

3 Sew each fabric 6 strip to a fabric 7 strip along the long edges to make two strip set B and each fabric 8 strip to a fabric 9 strip to make two strip set C. Press the seam allowances in either direction. Crosscut each pair of strip sets into 16 segments, 2½" wide.

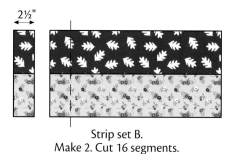

Strip set B.
Make 2. Cut 16 segments.

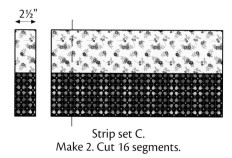

Strip set C.
Make 2. Cut 16 segments.

4 Sew a strip set B segment to the left edge and a strip set C segment to the right edge of each unit from step 2. Press the seam allowances away from the center.

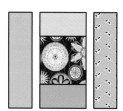

Make 16.

5 Sew each fabric 10 strip to a fabric 11 strip along the long edges to make two strip set D and each fabric 12 strip to a fabric 13 strip to make two strip set E. Press the seam allowances in either direction. Crosscut each pair of strip sets into 16 segments, 2½" wide.

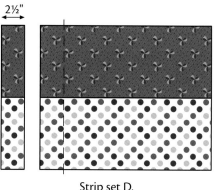

Strip set D.
Make 2. Cut 16 segments.

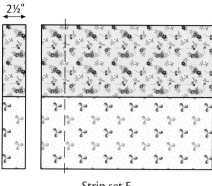

Strip set E.
Make 2. Cut 16 segments.

6 Sew a strip set D segment to the top edge and a strip set E segment to the bottom edge of each unit from step 4. Press the seam allowances away from the center.

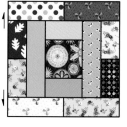

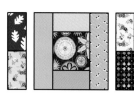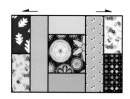

Make 16.

Assembling the Quilt Top

1 Refer to the quilt assembly diagram below to arrange the blocks into four rows of four blocks each, rotating every other block a quarter turn. Sew the blocks in each row together. Press the seam allowances in opposite directions from row to row. Sew the rows together. Press the seam allowances in one direction.

2 Refer to "Adding Borders" on page 59 to sew the border to the quilt top using the multicolored 7"-wide strips.

Finishing the Quilt

1 Layer the quilt top with batting and backing. Baste the layers together.

2 Hand or machine quilt as desired.

3 Square up the quilt sandwich.

4 Prepare and sew the binding to the quilt using the fat quarter 2½"-wide strips. Add a hanging sleeve, if desired, and a label.

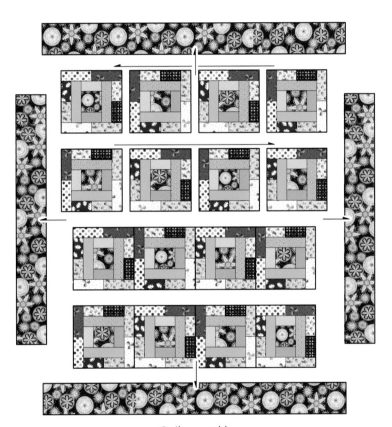

Quilt assembly

quick KIMONO

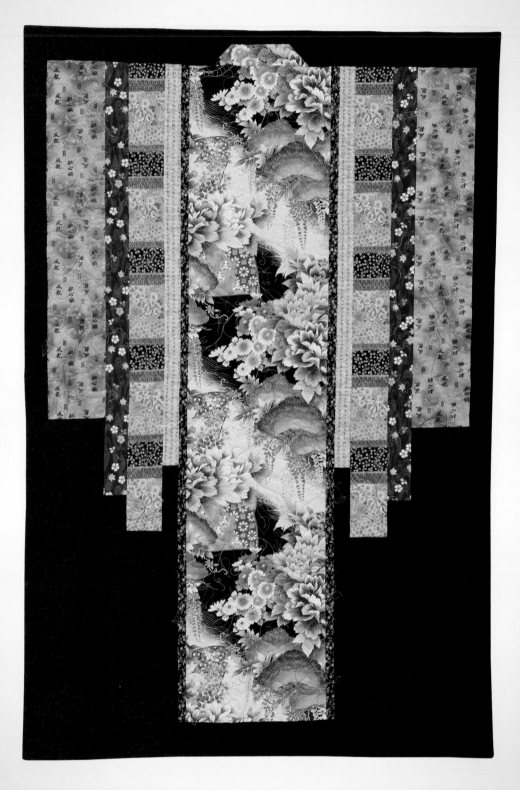

By Terry Martin. Machine quilted by the one-and-only Adrienne Reynolds.
Finished quilt: 45½" x 65½"

Asian prints are rich with color and design, but the prints can also be very large in scale, so how does a traditional quilter who cuts fabric into small pieces handle the large-scale print without demolishing the scenery? Easy—use the scenic fabric in a large panel to show it off!

I had 10 more fabrics that I was working with for this project, and I was getting nowhere. I had intended to make a wall quilt with some pieced and some plain panels of fabric. Yikes! What a mess—no resting place for the eyes, the color palette was all over the place, and the prints were fighting with each other. I needed another pair of eyes on this project, and my daughter and husband couldn't help this time because it was that big of a mess! Best friend to the rescue! Cornelia came over and talked me through my problems: too much fabric, too much color, and meandering blobs of fabric. The quilt needed symmetry and balance. Tossing out the pieced bits and over half of the fabric and focusing on the center panel did the trick. I should call this quilt "Phoenix Rising" because from the ashes of my original design came a beautiful quilt. Oh, and by the way, thanks bunches, C. You always have my back.

Materials

Yardage is based on 42"-wide fabric unless otherwise indicated.

1⁷⁄₈ yards of large-scale print for kimono center panel

1²⁄₃ yards of black print for background and binding

½ yard of pink print for kimono

⅓ yard of 44"-wide striped print for kimono*

¼ yard of green print for kimono

¼ yard of burgundy print for kimono

¼ yard of black-and-pink print for kimono

3 yards of fabric for backing

50" x 71" piece of batting

*If your fabric is not 44" wide, purchase ⅛ yard extra for piecing the strips.

Cutting

All measurements include ¼"-wide seam allowances.

From the *lengthwise grain* of the large-scale print, cut:
1 strip, 14" x 60"
1 rectangle, 2½" x 10"

From the black-and-pink print, cut:
3 strips, 1¼" x 42"

From the green print, cut:
2 strips, 2" x 37¾"

From the striped print, cut:
2 strips, 4" x 43½" (if your fabric was not 44" wide, add extra length to each strip, matching the pattern, and trim to the exact length)

From the burgundy print, cut:
2 strips, 2¾" x 40¼"

From the pink print, cut:
2 strips, 6½" x 33½"

From the black print, cut:
1 strip, 3½" x 15½"
2 strips, 2" x 25¾"
2 strips, 4" x 20"
2 strips, 2¾" x 23¼"
2 strips, 6½" x 30"
4 strips, 2½" x 42"
2 squares, 2½" x 2½"
1 strip, 1½" x 10"
2 strips, 3½" x 18½"
6 strips, 2¼" x 42"

Assembling the Quilt Top

Refer to the quilt assembly diagram below. Press all seam allowances away from the center rectangle unless otherwise indicated.

1 Sew the black-and-pink 1¼" x 42" strips together end to end to make one long strip. From the pieced strip, cut two strips, 1¼" x 60". Sew these strips to the sides of the large-scale print 14" x 60" rectangle.

2 Join the black print 3½" x 15½" rectangle to the bottom of the unit created in step 1.

3 Sew a black print 2" x 25¾" strip to the end of each green print 2" x 37¾" strip. Sew these strips to the sides of the unit from step 2.

4 Join a black print 4" x 20" strip to the end of each striped 4" x 43½" strip. Add these strips to the sides of the unit from step 3.

5 Sew a black print 2¾" x 23¼" strip to the end of each burgundy 2¾" x 40¼" strip. Join these strips to the sides of the unit from step 4.

6 Join a black print 6½" x 30" strip to the end of each pink print 6½" x 33½" strip. Add these strips to the sides of the unit from step 5.

7 Sew the black print 2½" x 42" strips together end to end to make one long strip. From the pieced strip, cut two strips, 2½" x 63". Sew these strips to the sides of the unit from step 6.

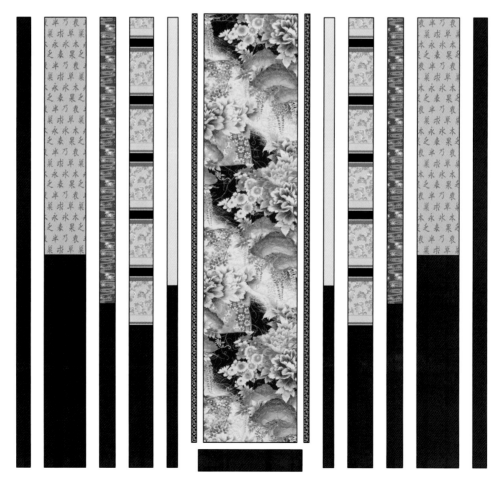

8 Draw a diagonal line from corner to corner on the wrong side of each black print 2½" square. With right sides together, position a square on each end of the large-scale print 2½" x 10" rectangle as shown. Sew on the marked lines. Trim ¼" from the stitching lines. Press the resulting triangle toward the corners.

9 Sew the black print 1½" x 10" rectangle to the top of the unit created in step 8.

Consider developing the Japanese theme further by using traditional sashiko designs when quilting. Kitty Pippen's *Quilting with Japanese Fabrics* is a fascinating book full of beautiful sashiko motifs and great projects.

10 Add a black print 3½" x 18½" strip to each side of the unit created in step 9. Press the seam allowances toward the black strips. Sew this unit to the top of the unit from step 7.

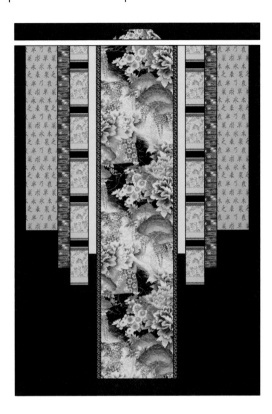

Finishing the Quilt

1 Layer the quilt top with batting and backing. Baste the layers together.

2 Hand or machine quilt as desired.

3 Square up the quilt sandwich.

4 Prepare and sew the binding to the quilt using the black print 2¼"-wide strips. Add a hanging sleeve, if desired, and a label.

simply CHARMING

By Terry Martin. Machine quilted by the fast and fabulous Sue Lohse.

Finished quilt: 98½" x 98½" • **Finished block:** 5½" x 5½"

I belong to the Busy Bee Quilt Guild of Snohomish, Washington, and we've been exchanging 6" fabric squares for years. Every month a different fabric theme is announced so you can pick and choose when you want to participate. I have partici-pated in many of the exchanges, so I had enough squares to pick and choose from to create this quilt. I sorted through the squares and created a pile of bright tone-on-tone squares and a pile of black-and-white prints. This quilt is fun to make, super easy, and you can easily adapt it to any size you want, depending on how many squares you have or fabrics you want to include. You can even change the size of the squares.

Materials

Yardage is based on 42"-wide fabric.

5 yards *total* or 187 squares, 6" x 6", of assorted black-and-white prints

4¼ yards *total* or 156 squares, 6" x 6", of bright tone-on-tone prints

⅞ yard of fabric for binding

8¾ yards of fabric for backing

104" x 104" piece of batting

CHARM SQUARES

Many fabric companies offer precut 5" charm squares, which you can also use for this quilt. For the sashing pieces, cut the squares in half to make 2½" x 5" rectangles and into quarters to make 2½" squares. The final dimensions of the quilt will be 80" x 80".

Cutting

All measurements include ¼"-wide seam allowances.

From the black-and-white prints, cut:

187 squares, 6" x 6"; cut 43 squares into quarters to yield 172 squares, 3" x 3" (you will use 169)

From the bright tone-on-tone prints, cut:

156 squares, 6" x 6"; cut in half to yield 312 rectangles, 3" x 6"

From the binding fabric, cut:

11 strips, 2½" x 42"

Assembling the Quilt Top

1 Sew a bright tone-on-tone rectangle to one side of each black-and-white print 6" square. Make 144. Press the seam allowances toward the rectangles.

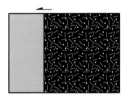

Make 144.

2 Sew 12 units from step 1 together side by side to make a block row. Add a bright tone-on-tone rectangle to the end of the row. Press the seam allowances toward the rectangles. Repeat to make a total of 12 rows.

Make 12 rows.

3 Sew a black-and-white 3" square to the short side of the remaining bright tone-on-tone rectangles. Make 156. Press the seam allowances toward the rectangles.

Make 156.

4 Sew 12 of the units from step 3 together end to end to make a sashing row. Add a black-and-white 3" square to the end of the row. Press the seam allowances toward the rectangles. Repeat to make a total of 13 rows.

Make 13 rows.

5 Refer to the quilt assembly diagram to alternately sew the sashing rows and block rows together. Press the seam allowances in one direction.

Finishing the Quilt

1 Layer the quilt top with batting and backing. Baste the layers together.

2 Hand or machine quilt as desired.

3 Square up the quilt sandwich.

4 Prepare and sew the binding to the quilt using the 2½"-wide strips of binding fabric. Add a hanging sleeve, if desired, and a label.

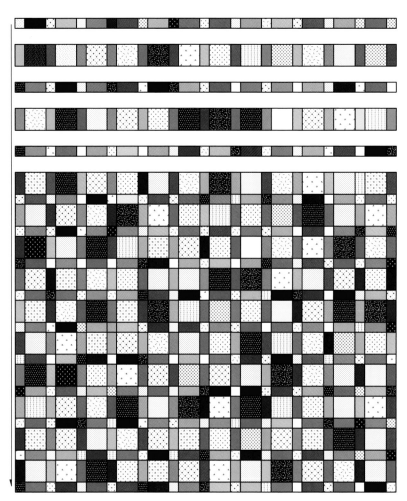

Quilt assembly

so, sew SIMPLE

By Terry Martin. Machine quilted by the fabulous Adrienne Reynolds.

Finished Quilt: 78" x 92" • **Finished Window blocks:** 5" x 5" • **Finished Flying Geese blocks:** 3" x 6"

I love, love, love the large-scale print I used in this quilt and wanted to show it off. The center panel really highlights the fabric and looks great on a bed. You could even take this quilt to the beach for some tropical fun in the sun. With a progression of borders, this quilt goes together really fast. The Window blocks and Flying Geese blocks add a lot of movement to the already splashy center, and using the large-scale print between the pieced borders makes them appear to float. A nice calm border of simple squares finishes up things nicely. This quilt would also be awesome if you used scraps for the pieced borders.

Materials

Yardage is based on 42"-wide fabric.

3½ yards of large-scale floral print for center panel, borders, and binding

1⅞ yards of orange-and-red batik for Flying Geese blocks and border squares

1⅛ yards of red batik for Flying Geese blocks and border squares

¾ yard of yellow print for Window blocks

½ yard of green batik for Window blocks and border squares

½ yard of dark blue batik for Window blocks and border squares

½ yard of dark pink batik for Window blocks and border squares

¼ yard of blue batik for border squares

¼ yard of orange print batik for border squares

¼ yard of coral batik for border squares

7¼ yards of fabric for backing

86" x 103" piece of batting

Cutting

All measurements include a ¼"-wide seam allowance.

From *each* of the dark blue and dark pink batiks, cut:

3 strips, 2½" x 42" (6 total)

1 strip, 4½" x 42" (2 total)

From the green batik, cut:

7 strips, 1½" x 42"; crosscut 4 strips into 24 rectangles, 1½" x 5½"

1 strip, 4½" x 42"

From the red batik, cut:

8 strips, 3⅞" x 42"; crosscut into 74 squares, 3⅞" x 3⅞". Cut each square in half diagonally to yield 148 triangles.

1 strip, 4½" x 42"

From the orange-and-red batik, cut:

4 strips, 7¼" x 42"; crosscut into 19 squares, 7¼" x 7¼". Cut each square into quarters diagonally to yield 76 triangles (you will use 74).

1 strip, 6½" x 42"; crosscut into 4 squares, 6½" x 6½"

1 strip, 4½" x 42"

9 strips, 2¼" x 42"

From the large-scale floral print, cut:

1 rectangle, 28½" x 42½"

13 strips, 3½" x 42"

8 strips, 2½" x 42"

4 squares, 4½" x 4½"

From the yellow print, cut:

7 strips, 1½" x 42"

2 strips, 1½" x 30½"

4 strips, 2½" x 42"; crosscut into 24 rectangles, 2½" x 5½"

From *each* of the blue, coral, and orange print batiks, cut:

1 strip, 4½" x 42" (3 total)

Making the Border Blocks

1 To make the Window blocks, sew a dark pink and a dark blue 2½" x 42" strip to the long edges of a green batik 1½" x 42" strip to make a strip set. Repeat to make a total of three strip sets. Press the seam allowances toward the pink and blue strips. Crosscut the strip sets into 48 segments, 2½" wide.

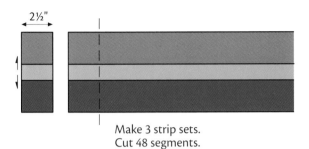

2½"

Make 3 strip sets.
Cut 48 segments.

2 Join segments from step 1 to both long edges of each green batik 1½" x 5½" rectangle. Make 24.

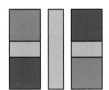

Make 24.

3 To make the Flying Geese blocks, sew red batik triangles to both long edges of 74 orange-and-red batik triangles. Press the seam allowances toward the red triangles.

Make 74.

Assembling the Quilt Top

Refer to the quilt assembly diagram on page 41.

1 Sew the yellow print 1½" x 42" strips together end to end to make one long strip. From the pieced strip, cut two strips, 1½" x 42½". Sew these strips to the sides of the large-scale print 28½" x 42½" rectangle. Press the seam allowances toward the border. Sew the yellow print 1½" x 30½" strips to the top and bottom of the rectangle. Press the seam allowances toward the border. Set the remainder of the pieced strip aside.

2 Alternately sew together six Window blocks and seven yellow print 2½" x 5½" rectangles. Press the seam allowances toward the rectangles. Repeat to make a total of two border rows. Sew these borders to the sides of the center panel unit from step 1. Press the seam allowances toward the yellow print border. Sew six Window blocks and five yellow print 2½" x 5½" rectangles together. Press the seam allowances toward the rectangles. Repeat to make a total of two border rows. Sew these borders to the top and bottom of the center panel unit. Press the seam allowances toward the yellow print border.

Side border.
Make 2.

Top/bottom border.
Make 2.

3 From the remainder of the pieced yellow strip, cut two segments, 1½" x 54½", and sew them to the sides of the quilt top. Press the seam allowances toward the newly added border. Cut two more strips from the pieced yellow strip, 1½" x 42½", and sew them to the top and bottom of the quilt top. Press the seam allowances toward the newly added border.

4 Sew the large-scale floral 3½" x 42" strips together end to end to make one long strip. From the pieced strip, cut two strips, 3½" x 56½". Join these strips to the sides of the quilt top. Press the seam allowances toward the newly added border. From the remainder of the pieced strip, cut two strips, 3½" x 48½". Sew these strips to the top and bottom of the quilt top. Press the seam allowances toward the newly added border. Set the remainder of the pieced strip aside.

5 Sew 21 Flying Geese blocks together side by side. Make sure all the geese are flying in the same direction, or mix it up if you prefer! Press the seam allowances in one direction. Repeat to make a total of two rows. Sew these rows to the sides of the quilt top, paying careful attention to the direction the geese are flying. Press the seam allowances toward the large-scale floral border. Sew 16 Flying Geese blocks together in the same manner. Repeat to make a total of two rows. Add an orange-and-red batik 6½" square to each end of each row. Press the seam allowances toward the squares. Join these rows to the top and bottom of the quilt top, again watching the direction the geese are flying. Press the seam allowances toward the large-scale floral border.

Side border.
Make 2.

Top/bottom border.
Make 2.

6 Join the large-scale floral 2½" x 42" strips end to end to make one long strip. From the pieced strip, cut two strips, 2½" x 75½". Add these strips to the sides of the quilt top. Press the seam allowances

toward the newly added borders. From the remainder of the pieced strip, cut two strips, 2½" x 60½", and add them to the top and bottom of the quilt top. Press the seam allowances toward the newly added borders.

7 Sew the 4½" x 42" strips of dark blue batik, dark pink batik, green batik, orange-and-red batik, red batik, blue print, coral print, and orange print along the long edges to make a strip set. Press the seam allowances in one direction. Crosscut the strip set into nine segments, 4½" wide.

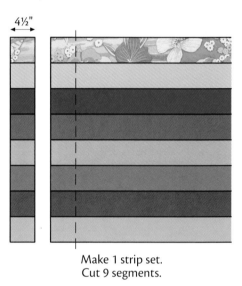

Make 1 strip set.
Cut 9 segments.

8 Sew two segments from step 7 together end to end so that the colors alternate in the same sequence. Repeat to make a total of four strips. Unsew the remaining segment at the halfway point to make two segments of four squares each. Sew a half segment to two of the four strips. Sew these strips to the sides of the quilt top. Press the seam allowances toward the large-scale floral border. To both ends of the two remaining strips, add a large-scale print 4½" square. Join these strips to the top and bottom of the quilt top. Press the seam allowances toward the large-scale floral border.

9 Refer to "Adding Borders" on page 59 to add the outer border to the quilt top using the remainder of the pieced large-scale floral 3½"-wide strip. Press the seam allowances toward the newly added border.

Finishing the Quilt

1 Layer the quilt top with batting and backing. Baste the layers together.

2 Hand or machine quilt as desired.

3 Square up the quilt sandwich.

4 Prepare and sew the binding to the quilt using the orange-and-red batik 2¼"-wide strips. Add a hanging sleeve, if desired, and a label.

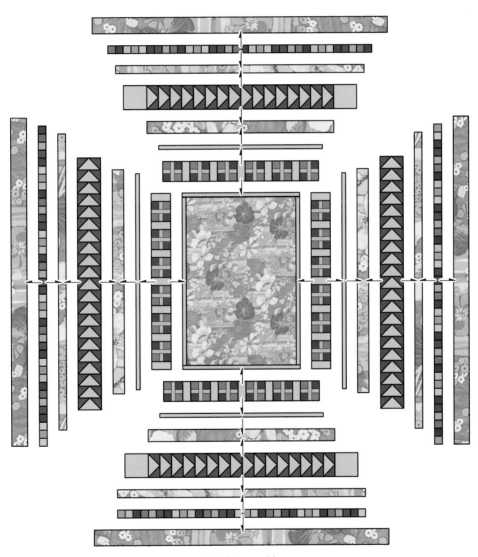

Quilt assembly

ocean WAVES

By Terry Martin. Machine quilted by the awesome Adrienne Reynolds.

Finished quilt: 56¾" x 56¾" • **Finished block:** 4¾" x 4¾"

I like to make Hourglass blocks—you know, a square made from four triangles. They're simple and very easy to make, and if you stack your fat quarters and cut all the pieces at once, you'll save loads of time, too. The seams that come together in the center always match perfectly when you follow this tip: Before sewing the two pieced triangle units together that make the Hourglass block, match up the center seam first. Because the seams are going in opposition directions, they will "lock" together and you will have perfectly matching seams in the center. Making the Ocean Waves pattern using Hourglass blocks and plain squares eliminates matching additional seams, and you'll have a successfully constructed quilt that is dynamic looking with lots of movement!

Materials

Yardage is based on 42"-wide fabric.

10 fat quarters of assorted batik solids for blocks

1⅓ yards of solid blue batik for blocks and borders

½ yard of fabric for binding

3½ yards of fabric for backing

63" x 63" piece of batting

Cutting

All measurements include ¼"-wide seam allowances.

From the solid blue batik, cut:

8 strips, 5¼" x 42"; crosscut into:
   4 strips, 5¼" x 38¼"
   24 squares, 5¼" x 5¼"

From each of the 10 fat quarters, cut:

8 squares, 6" x 6"; cut into quarters diagonally to yield 320 triangles (you will use 292)

3 squares, 4¼" x 4¼"; cut in half diagonally to yield 60 triangles (you will use 52)

From the binding fabric, cut:

7 strips, 2¼" x 42"

Making the Blocks

1 Randomly select and sew together two 6" triangles along the short edges as shown. Repeat to make a total of 146 triangle units. Do not press the seam allowances yet.

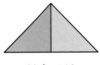

Make 146.

2 Randomly select two triangle units from step 1. Press the seam allowance of one unit in one direction and the seam allowance of the other unit in the opposite direction. Sew the units together to complete the Hourglass block. Repeat to make a total of 73 blocks.

Make 73.

Assembling the Quilt Top

1 Randomly sew together two 4¼" triangles along the short edges as shown. Repeat to make a total of 24 pieced side setting triangles. The remaining four triangles are the corner triangles.

Make 24.

2 Set aside 12 Hourglass blocks for the border. Refer to the quilt assembly below to arrange the remaining blocks, the blue batik 5¼" squares, and the side setting triangles into diagonal rows. Sew the pieces in each row together. Press the seam allowances in opposite directions from row to row. Sew the rows together. Press the seam allowances away from the center row. Add the corner triangles last. Press the seam allowances toward the triangles.

3 Sew Hourglass blocks to both ends of each blue batik 5¼" x 38¼" strip. Press the seam allowances toward the strip. Sew two of these strips to the sides of the quilt top. Press the seam allowances toward the border. Add an Hourglass block to both ends of the remaining two strips. Sew these strips to the top and bottom of the quilt top. Press the seam allowances toward the border.

Finishing the Quilt

1 Layer the quilt top with batting and backing. Baste the layers together.

2 Hand or machine quilt as desired.

3 Square up the quilt sandwich.

4 Prepare and sew the binding to the quilt using the 2¼"-wide strips of binding fabric. Add a hanging sleeve, if desired, and a label.

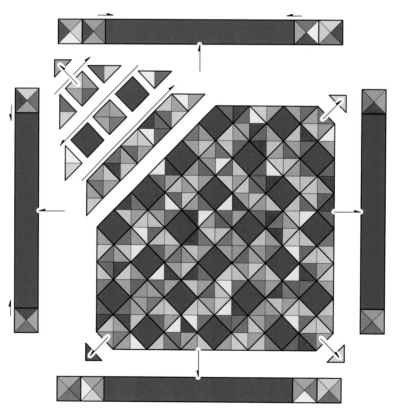

Quilt assembly

spice of LIFE

By Terry Martin. Machine quilted by the fabulous Barb Dau.

Finished quilt: 52" x 64" • **Finished Star blocks:** 12" x 12" • **Finished Border blocks:** 4" x 4"

I collect salt and pepper shakers—some are new and remind me of the places I've visited and some are vintage. So, when I found this salt-and-pepper-shaker print fabric with its retro look, I knew I had to have it. The colors in the print were used to select the coordinating tone-on-tone fabrics. When choosing coordinating fabric from a main print, use the color dots printed on the selvage that show all of the colors that were used in the printing process. It's a great way to check your colors so they coordinate well.

Materials

Yardage is based on 42"-wide fabric.

½ yard *each* of 6 coordinating tone-on-tone fabrics for blocks

2½ yards of novelty print for blocks and inner border

½ yard of fabric for binding

3¼ yards of fabric for backing

58" x 70" piece of batting

Cutting

All measurements include ¼"-wide seam allowances.

From *each* of the 6 coordinating tone-on-tone fabrics, cut:

2 strips, 5¼" x 42"; crosscut into 10 squares, 5¼" x 5¼". Cut each square into quarters diagonally to yield 40 triangles (240 total; you will use 208).

1 strip, 4½" x 42"; crosscut into 5 squares, 4½" x 4½" (30 total; you will use 26)

From the novelty print, cut:

13 strips, 4½" x 42"; crosscut 8 strips into 60 squares, 4½" x 4½"

4 strips, 5¼" x 42"; crosscut into 24 squares, 5¼" x 5¼". Cut each square into quarters diagonally to yield 96 triangles.

From the binding fabric, cut:

7 strips, 2¼" x 42

Making the Blocks

1 To make the Star blocks, sew a novelty print 5¼" triangle to each of 16 matching tone-on-tone 5¼" triangles, sewing along the short edges to make a triangle unit. Press the seam allowances toward the solid triangles.

Make 16.

2 Sew two triangle units from step 1 together as shown to make an hourglass unit. Repeat to make a total of eight hourglass units.

Make 8.

3 Arrange four hourglass units and five novelty print 4½" squares into three vertical rows. Sew the pieces in each row together. Press the seam allowances toward the novelty squares. Sew the rows together. Press the seam allowances toward the top and bottom rows. Repeat to make a total of two blocks.

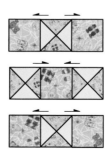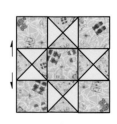

Make 2.

4 Repeat steps 1–3 to make two blocks from each of the remaining five tone-on-tone fabrics (12 total blocks).

5 To make the border blocks, randomly select four different tone-on-tone fabrics 5¼" triangles. Sew two triangles together along the short edges. Repeat for the remaining two triangles. Sew the pieced triangles together, pressing the seam allowances in opposite directions so they oppose each other when sewn together. Repeat to make a total of 28 blocks.

Make 28.

Assembling the Quilt Top

1 Refer to the quilt assembly diagram to randomly arrange the Star blocks into four rows of three blocks each. Sew the blocks in each row together. Press the seam allowances in opposite directions from row to row. Sew the rows together. Press the seam allowances in one direction.

2 Sew the novelty print 4½" x 42" strips together end to end to make one long strip. From the pieced strip, cut two inner-border strips, 4½" x 48½". Sew these strips to the sides of the quilt top. Press the seam allowances toward the border strips. From the remainder of the pieced strip, cut two strips, 4½" x 44½". Sew these strips to the top and bottom edges of the quilt top. Press the seam allowances toward the border strips.

3 Randomly select seven tone-on-tone squares and seven border blocks. Alternately sew the pieces together. Press the seam allowances toward the tone-on-tone squares. Repeat to make a total of two border strips. Sew the borders to the sides of the quilt top, making sure the tone-on-tone square is at the top on one side and at the bottom on the other side. Press the seam allowances toward the

inner border. Randomly select seven border blocks and six tone-on-tone squares. Alternately sew the pieces together. Press the seam allowances toward the tone-on-tone squares. Repeat to make a total of two border strips. Sew the borders to the top and bottom of the quilt top. Press the seam allowances toward the inner border.

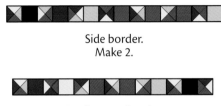

Side border.
Make 2.

Top/bottom border.
Make 2.

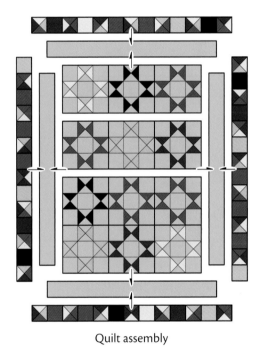

Quilt assembly

Finishing the Quilt

1 Layer the quilt top with batting and backing. Baste the layers together.

2 Hand or machine quilt as desired.

3 Square up the quilt sandwich.

4 Prepare and sew the binding to the quilt using the 2¼"-wide strips of binding fabric. Add a hanging sleeve, if desired, and a label.

charming SQUARES AND DIAMONDS

By Terry Martin.

Finished quilt: 27" x 36" • **Finished block:** 4½" x 4½"

I enjoy shopping for and using charm packs, bundles of 5" squares of fabric. They give me the opportunity to see which fabrics I want more yardage of without investing a lot of money. For this quilt, I supplemented a pack of romantic Victorian-style florals with fabric from my stash. (Excuse me, I meant to say "collection." It sounds less intimidating— at least to my husband!)

I free-form cut the diamond shapes using a rotary cutter and scissors, and then used a decorative machine stitch to secure the raw edges after the quilt layers were assembled. The decorative stitching also serves to quilt the layers together. I got this idea from Judy Irish, friend, world-renowned machine quilter, and fellow guild member.

Materials

Yardage is based on 42"-wide fabric.

48 assorted light print charm squares, 5" x 5", for background*

⅝ yards of medium to dark tone-on-tone print for diamond appliqués and binding

1 yard of fabric for backing

33" x 42" piece of batting

1⅓ yards of 12"-wide lightweight paper-backed fusible web (I used Steam-A-Seam 2)

You can also cut your own squares from yardage or scraps.

Cutting

The measurement includes a ¼"-wide seam allowance.

From the tone-on-tone print, cut:

4 strips, 2¼" x 42"

Assembling the Quilt Top

1 Randomly arrange the 5" squares into eight rows of six squares each. Sew the square in each row together. Press the seam allowances in opposite directions from row to row. Sew the rows together. Press the seam allowances in one direction.

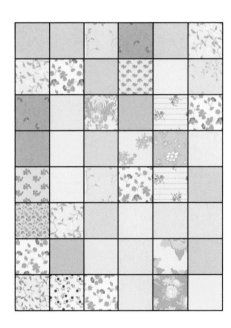

2 Layer the quilt top with batting and backing. Baste the layers together. Using a thread that blends with all of the fabrics, stitch in the ditch of all of the seams.

3 Follow the manufacturer's instructions to fuse the fusible web to the wrong side of the remaining piece of tone-on-tone fabric. From the fused fabric, cut 6 strips, 1½" wide. Crosscut the strips into 58 rectangles, 1½" x 4½".

4 Fold a rectangle in half along the long edges to make a piece 1½" x 2¼". Then fold the piece in half at the short raw edges and finger crease the fold to mark the center. Cut from the outside edge of the fold to the center mark on each side of the rectangle. Repeat with the remaining rectangles to make a total of 58 diamonds. Remove the paper backing from each diamond.

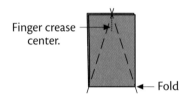

Finger crease center.

Fold

5 Place a diamond directly over every inside seam except those on the outer squares, with the points meeting at the intersections as shown. Refer to the

manufacturer's instructions to fuse the diamonds in place.

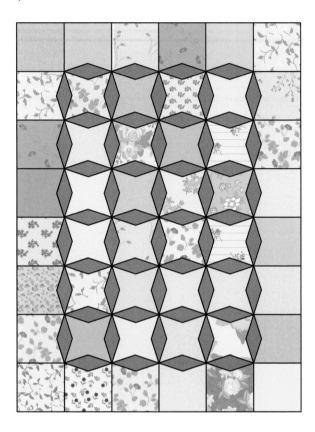

6 Using a decorative machine stitch, stitch over the raw edges of the diamonds. For best results sew down the side of one row, and then with the needle down, pivot 180° and sew the other half of the row. Start with the center row and work outward.

Finishing the Quilt

1 Add additional machine quilting if desired.

2 Square up the quilt sandwich.

3 Prepare and sew the binding to the quilt using the tone-on-tone 2¼"-wide strips. Add a hanging sleeve, if desired, and a label.

flower POWER

By Terry Martin. Machine quilted by the very talented Adrienne Reynolds.

Finished Quilt: 68" x 72½" • **Finished block:** 4½" x 4½"

This was a fun quilt to make and I like its whimsy. A friend gave me a huge stack of fat quarters, all from one line of fabric. The fat quarters had a contemporary flair to them and I thought this simple design would be perfect to show off the fabric. I used the rest of the pile of fat quarters for the backing.

The construction of this quilt includes stacking and cutting the fabric, because you cut the same units from each of the background fat quarters. You can then stack and cut the sewn strip pieces for even faster results. The appliqué work is minimal and uses easy shapes. Fused raw-edge appliqué is also quick—the sewing machine does all the work!

I had never made a yo-yo until I purchased a Quick Yo-Yo Maker by Clover. It's so easy! Of course you can use any method you like for making yo-yos—or simply use buttons for the flower centers.

Materials

Yardage is based on 42"-wide fabric.

13 assorted fat quarters for background

2⅛ yards of black floral print for border and binding

1 fat quarter *each* of 3 coordinating prints for flower, stem, and leaf appliqués

Scraps of fabric for flower centers

4¼ yards of fabric for backing

74" x 79" piece of batting

1⅞ yards of 18"-wide lightweight paper-backed fusible web (I used Steam-A-Seam 2)

45 mm and 60 mm yo-yo makers

9 yellow ½"-diameter buttons

Cutting

All measurements include ¼"-wide seam allowances.

From *each* of the 13 background fat quarters, cut:

3 strips, 5" x the longest edge of the fat quarter (39 total)

From the black floral print, cut:

7 strips, 7½" x 42"

8 strips, 2¼" x 42"

Assembling the Quilt Top

1 Randomly select three different background strips and sew them together along the long edges to make a strip set. Press the seam allowances in one direction. Repeat to make a total of 13 strip sets. Crosscut *each* strip set into four segments, 5" wide (52 total).

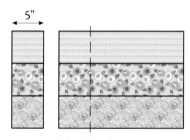

Make 13 strip sets.
Cut 4 segments from each (52 total).

2 Randomly select four segments and sew them together end to end to make a row, making sure all the seam allowances are pressed in the same direction. Repeat to make a total of 13 rows.

Make 13.

3 Join the rows, rotating the rows as needed so the seam allowances are pressed in opposite directions from row to row.

4 Using the patterns on pages 54 and 55, trace five large flower petal shapes, 10 medium flower petal shapes, and 35 stem/leaf shapes onto the paper side of the fusible web. Roughly cut around each shape. Follow the manufacturer's instructions to fuse the five large flower petals shapes and 15 of the stem/leaf shapes to the wrong side of one of the coordinating fat quarters. Cut out the shapes on the marked lines. Cut the stem/leaf shapes in half lengthwise along the center cutting line. Fuse the 10 medium flower petal shapes to a different coordinating fat quarter and fuse the 20 remaining stem/leaf shapes to the remaining coordinating fat quarter. Cut out the shapes on the marked lines. Remove the paper backing from all of the pieces.

5 Referring to the photo on page 51 and the quilt assembly diagram below, arrange the shapes on the quilt top as shown or create your own unique arrangement. When you're satisfied with the results, fuse the shapes in place.

6 Using a narrow zigzag stitch, hem stitch, or a decorative machine stitch, stitch around the outer edges of each fused shape. This is recommended if the quilt will be laundered frequently and not simply hung as a wall hanging.

7 Refer to "Adding Borders" on page 59 to sew the borders to the quilt top using the black floral 7½"-wide strips.

Finishing the Quilt

1 Layer the quilt top with batting and backing. Baste the layers together.

2 Hand or machine quilt as desired.

3 Square up the quilt sandwich.

4 Prepare and sew the binding to the quilt using the black floral 2¼"-wide strips. Add a hanging sleeve, if desired, and a label.

5 Follow the manufacturer's instructions included with the yo-yo maker to make one large and two small yo-yos from the fabric scraps. With the open side down, sew the large yo-yo to the center of the large flower and the small yo-yos to the center of the two small flowers. Sew three yellow buttons to the center of each yo-yo.

Quilt assembly

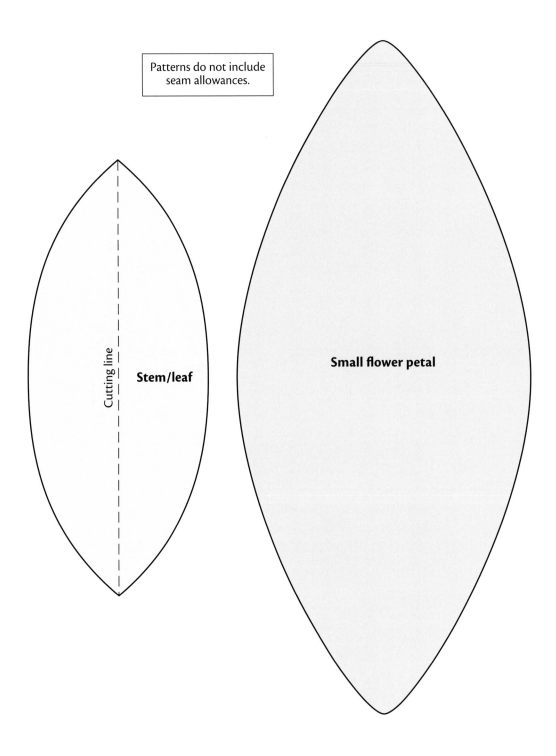

Patterns do not include
seam allowances.

Cutting line

Stem/leaf

Small flower petal

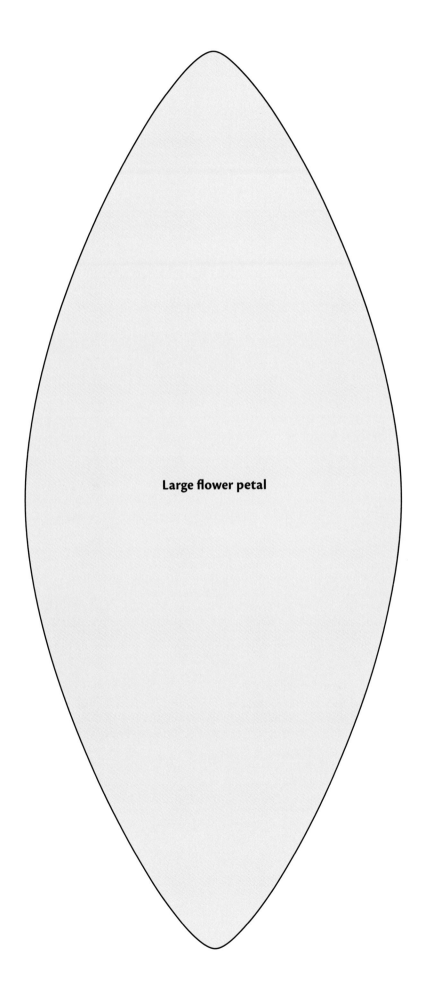

Large flower petal

quiltmaking BASICS

This section provides you with a brief explanation of all the necessary elements for successfully completing your project, from choosing fabric and assembling essential tools for quiltmaking to chain piecing, pressing, adding borders, making a quilt sandwich, quilting, binding, and finally adding a hanging sleeve and label.

Fabrics

I use 100% cotton fabric. I like to buy fabrics from quilt shops; they generally carry the best quality of cotton goods. Buy fabric, make things, and enjoy your accomplishments! Yardage requirements are provided for all projects in this book and are based on 42" of usable fabric.

Supplies

Sewing machine. You'll need a sewing machine that has a good straight stitch. You'll also need a walking foot or darning foot if you're going to machine quilt.

Rotary-cutting tools. Rotary-cutting techniques are used throughout the book, so you'll need a rotary cutter, cutting mat, and a clear acrylic ruler. The 6" x 24" ruler size works well for cutting long strips and squares.

Thread. Use a good-quality, all-purpose cotton or cotton-covered-polyester thread. Choose a neutral color such as gray for less chance of show through when you're piecing light and dark fabrics together.

Basic sewing tools. Hand- and machine-sewing needles, pins, and fabric scissors for cutting threads are all necessary items to have on hand. Don't forget the seam ripper—the smaller the better so the point can slide through the stitches easily. An iron and ironing board are needed for pressing seams, and tracing tools such as pencil and paper are used for the appliqué projects.

Paper-backed fusible webbing. I use double-sided Steam-a-Seam 2 by the Warm Company. It holds very well and adds just enough body to the fabric without being so stiff that I have to use a stabilizer when I machine stitch around the edges of fused designs.

Rotary Cutting

All of the projects are designed for quick-and-easy rotary cutting, except those involving fusible appliqué. All measurements, except those given for template-free appliqué, include standard ¼"-wide seam allowances. Here is a quick lesson on rotary cutting.

1 Fold the fabric in half widthwise, matching the selvage edges and aligning the crosswise and lengthwise grains as much as possible. Place the folded edge closest to you on the cutting mat. Align the bottom edge of a square ruler along the folded edge of the fabric. Then place a long, straight ruler to the left of the square ruler, just covering the uneven raw edges of the left side of the fabric.

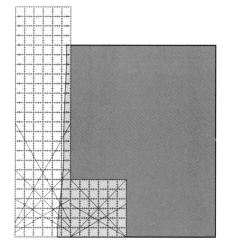

Remove the square ruler and cut along the right edge of the long ruler, rolling the rotary cutter away from you and using the inchworm technique described at right. Discard this strip. (Reverse this procedure if you are left-handed.)

2 To cut strips, align the required measurement on the ruler with the newly cut edge of the fabric. For example, to cut a 3"-wide strip, place the 3" ruler mark on the edge of the fabric.

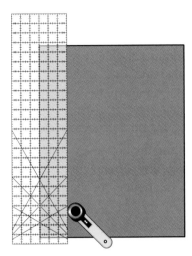

3 To cut squares or rectangles, cut strips in the required widths. Trim away the selvage ends of the strip. Align the required measurement on the ruler with the left edge of the strip and cut the piece. Continue cutting pieces until you have the number you need.

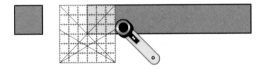

INCHWORM TECHNIQUE

When you're ready to make the first cut, place your ruler hand about a quarter of the way up the ruler, pressing straight down with you fingertips only, not your palm. Cut from the bottom of the ruler up to the point where you are parallel with the ruler hand; stop cutting but do not remove the rotary cutter from the fabric. Walk your fingers up the ruler about 6" and then cut until you're parallel with your ruler hand again. Repeat this process the width of the fabric. Believe me, keeping pressure on the portion of fabric you're cutting really helps with accuracy and you won't get that little wobbly bit at the end of the strip.

Machine Piecing

The most important thing to remember about machine piecing is to maintain a consistent scant ¼"-wide seam allowance. Some sewing machines have a special ¼" foot that measures exactly ¼" from the center needle position to the edge of the foot. This feature allows you to use the edge of the presser foot to guide the fabric for a perfect ¼"-wide seam allowance.

If your machine doesn't have such a foot, create a seam guide by placing the edge of a piece of tape ¼" from the needle.

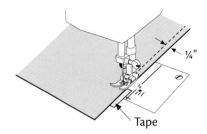

Tape

Chain Piecing

Chain piecing is an efficient, timesaving system.

1 Sew the first pair of pieces from cut edge to cut edge using about 12 stitches per inch. At the end of the seam, stop sewing but do not cut the thread.

2 Feed the next pair of pieces under the presser foot, as close as possible to the first pair. Continue feeding pieces through the machine without cutting the thread in between. There is no need to backstitch because each seam will be crossed and held by another seam.

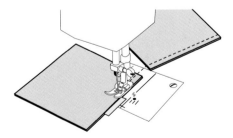

3 When all pieces have been sewn, remove the chain from the machine and clip the threads between pieces.

Easing

If two pieces that will be sewn together differ slightly in size (by less than ⅛"), pin the places where the two pieces should match. Next, pin the middle, if necessary, to distribute the excess fabric evenly. Sew the seam with the longer piece on the bottom, next to the feed dogs. The feed dogs will help ease the two pieces together.

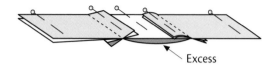

Excess

Pressing

Pressing is very important for several reasons: It helps sink the thread into the fabric, it sets the seam, and it helps you see if the pieces are stitched accurately.

The traditional rule in quiltmaking is to press seam allowances to one side, toward the darker color wherever possible. Press the seam flat from the wrong side first, and then press the seam allowances in the desired direction from the right side. Be particularly careful when pressing bias seams or edges.

When joining two seamed units, plan ahead and press the seam allowances in the opposite directions as shown. This reduces bulk and makes it easier to match seam lines. Where two seams meet, the seam allowances will butt against each other, making it easier to join units with perfectly matched seam intersections.

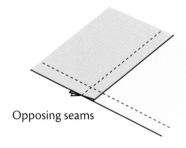

Opposing seams

Appliqué the Fusible Way

I want my projects to be quick and easy, so I use double-stick pressure-sensitive fusible webbing for the appliqué projects in this book. Please use your favorite appliqué method. The templates given do not have seam allowances.

If you do use double-stick fusible webbing, follow the manufacturer's instructions. For any project that will be handled a lot you will need to anchor the edges of the appliqué so they won't lift up with repeated washing. I use my sewing machine's preprogrammed blanket stitch to secure the appliqué to the background fabric. You can also use a blind hem stitch, narrow zigzag, satin stitch, or another decorative stitch.

Blanket stitch

Blind hem stitch

Satin stitch

Adding Borders

For best results, do not cut border strips and sew them directly to the quilt sides without measuring first, unless the quilt is small like a wall hanging. The edges of a quilt often measure slightly longer than the distance through the quilt center due to stretching during construction. Instead, measure the quilt top through the center in both directions to determine how long to cut the border strips. Then sew the strips to the edges of the quilt, easing to fit. This step ensures that the finished quilt will be as straight and as "square" as possible, without wavy edges.

Plain border strips are cut along the crosswise grain and seamed where extra length is needed.

All of the borders in this book have butted corners or have pieced details. For the detailed borders please follow the instructions given with the individual project. For borders with butted corners, follow these instructions.

1 Measure the length of the quilt top through the center. Cut border strips to that measurement, piecing as necessary. Mark the center of the quilt edges and the border strips. Pin the borders to the sides of the quilt top, matching the center marks and ends and easing as necessary. Sew the border strips in place. Press seam allowances toward the border.

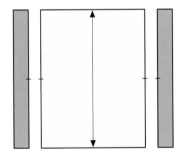

Measure center of quilt,
top to bottom. Mark centers.

2 Measure the width of the quilt top through the center, including the side borders just added. Cut border strips to that measurement, piecing as necessary; mark the center of the quilt edges and the border strips. Pin the borders to the top and bottom edges of the quilt top, matching the center marks

and ends and easing as necessary; stitch. Press seam allowances toward the border.

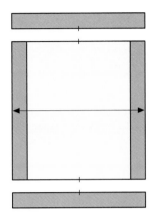

Measure center of quilt,
side to side, including borders.
Mark centers.

Layering the Quilt

The quilt "sandwich" consists of backing, batting, and the quilt top. Cut the quilt backing at least 4" larger in both length and width than the quilt top. For large quilts, it is usually necessary to sew two or three lengths of fabric together to make a backing of the required size. Trim away the selvages before piecing the lengths together. Press seam allowances open to make quilting easier.

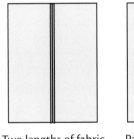

Two lengths of fabric   Partial fabric width
seamed in the center

Batting comes packaged in standard bed sizes, or it can be purchased by the yard. Several weights or thicknesses are available.

To put it all together, follow these steps.

1 Spread the backing, wrong side up, on a flat, clean surface. Anchor it with pins or masking tape. Be careful not to stretch the backing out of shape.

2   Spread the batting over the backing, smoothing out any wrinkles.

3   Place the pressed quilt top on top of the batting. Smooth out any wrinkles and make sure the quilt-top edges are parallel to the edges of the backing.

4   Starting in the center, baste with needle and thread and work diagonally to each corner. Continue basting in a grid of horizontal and vertical lines 6" to 8" apart. Finish by basting around the edges.

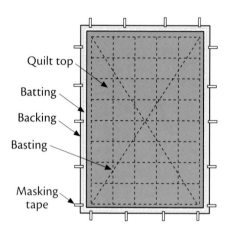

On smaller projects that I'm quilting by hand or machine, I have used an adhesive spray-basting product. There are several brands available, but my favorite is 505 Spray and Fix; it doesn't produce toxic fumes and works very well.

Machine Quilting

Machine quilting is suitable for all types of quilts, from crib to full-size bed quilts. With machine quilting, you can quickly complete quilts and start that next project that is calling out to you.

Marking is only necessary if you need to follow a grid or a complex pattern. It's not necessary if you plan to quilt in the ditch, outline quilt a uniform distance from seam lines, or free-motion quilt in a random pattern over the quilt surface or in selected areas.

For straight-line quilting, it's extremely helpful to have a walking foot to help feed the quilt layers through the machine without shifting or puckering. Some machines have a built-in walking foot; other machines require a separate attachment.

Walking foot

Quilting in the ditch   Outline quilting

For free-motion quilting, you need a darning foot and the ability to drop the feed dogs on your machine. With free-motion quilting, you do not turn the fabric under the needle but instead guide the fabric in the direction of the design. Use free-motion quilting to outline quilt a fabric motif or to create stippling or other curved designs.

Binding

Bindings can be made from straight-grain or bias strips of fabric. All of the quilts in this book call for a French double-fold binding.

To cut straight-grain binding strips, cut strips the width specified in the instructions across the width of the fabric. You will need enough strips to go around the perimeter of the quilt plus 10" for seams and the corners in a mitered fold.

1   With right sides together, join strips at right angles to make one long binding strip. Trim ¼" from the stitching lines and press the seam allowances open.

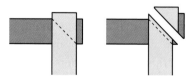

Joining straight-cut strips

2 Trim one end of the strip at a 45° angle, turn under ¼", and press. Trimming the end under at an angle distributes the bulk so you won't have a lump where the two ends of the binding meet. Fold the strip in half lengthwise, wrong sides together, and press.

Fold line

3 Trim the batting and backing even with the quilt top. If you plan to add a hanging sleeve, do so now before attaching the binding (see "Add a Hanging Sleeve" at right).

4 Starting on one side of the quilt and leaving about a 6" tail, stitch the binding to the quilt. Keep the raw edges even with the quilt-top edge and use a ¼" seam allowance. End the stitching ¼" from the corner of the quilt and backstitch. Clip the thread.

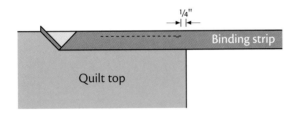

¼"

Binding strip

Quilt top

5 Turn the quilt so that you'll be stitching down the next side. Fold the binding up, away from the quilt, and then back down onto itself, parallel with the edge of the quilt top. Begin stitching at the edge; backstitching to secure. Repeat on the remaining edges and corners of the quilt.

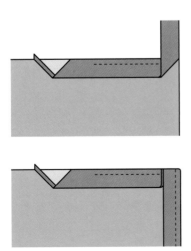

6 When you reach the beginning of the binding, overlap the end of the binding with the beginning stitches by 1" and cut away any excess binding, trimming the end at a 45° angle. Tuck the end of the binding into the fold and finish the seam.

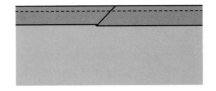

7 Fold the binding over the raw edges of the quilt to the back, with the folded edge covering the row of machine stitching, and blindstitch in place. A miter will form at each corner. Blindstitch the mitered corners.

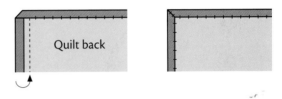

Quilt back

Add a Hanging Sleeve

If you plan to display your finished quilt on the wall, be sure to add a hanging sleeve to hold the rod before adding the binding. You can use leftover backing fabric or one of the fabrics from the quilt top.

1 Cut an 8"-wide strip of fabric that is equal to the width of your quilt. Press under each short end of the strip ½" twice. Stitch along the folded edges to create a hem.

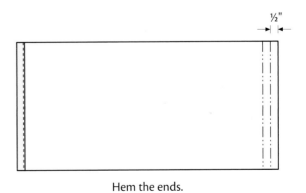

½"

Hem the ends.

2 Fold the strip in half lengthwise, wrong sides together. Center the strip at the top edge on the back of your quilt, aligning the raw edges, and baste it in place. The sleeve will be secured when the binding is stitched in place.

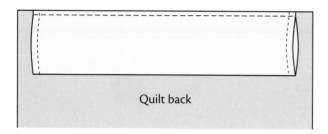

Quilt back

3 After the quilt is bound, slipstitch the bottom edges of the sleeve to the quilt back, making sure you don't stitch through to the front.

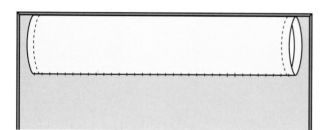

Signing Your Quilt

Be sure to sign and date your quilt. Future generations will be interested to know more than just who made it and when. Labels can be as elaborate or as simple as you desire. The information can be handwritten, typed, or embroidered. Be sure to include the name of the quilt, your name, your city and state, the date, the name of the recipient if it is a gift, and any other interesting or important information about the quilt.

Spice of Life
Made by Terry Martin
Snohomish, WA 2009
Quilted by Barb Dau

about the AUTHOR

Terry Martin leads a blessed life with the love of her family and friends. She belongs to several quilt groups that bring her joy, creativity, and simply the good fortune to hang out with some pretty incredibly talented women she calls friends.

She has been seriously quilting for about 12 years, and before that she was an avid cross-stitcher who dabbled in crewel and embroidery work and who made most of her own clothes. This is Terry's seventh quilting book and she has many more ideas than time. She loves to lecture and teach classes, and she hopes to eventually translate more of her quilting patterns and ideas into books.

THERE'S MORE ONLINE!

Find more great books on quilting, knitting, crochet, and more at www.martingale-pub.com.

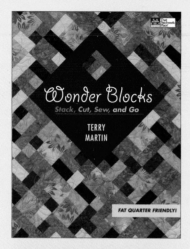
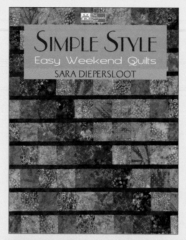

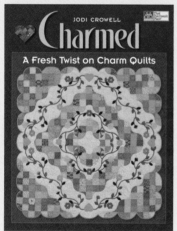

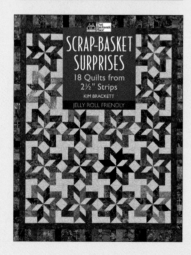

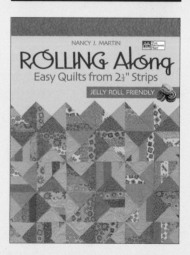